HOLY REVIVAL

Holy Revival

FINDING GOD'S LOVE THROUGH LIFE'S STORMS

Gibson Groft

Revival Fitness

Contents

Introduction

In the vast tapestry of existence, each thread weaves a unique story – a narrative of trials, triumphs, and the unyielding pursuit of purpose. My name is Gibson Groft, and I invite you to embark on a journey with me – a journey that transcends the chaos and challenges of life, a journey that echoes the profound love of our Creator. A goal of mine throughout this book is partly to develop a personal connection with you guys – the readers. I invite you to journey with me throughout these pages, and I ask that you would respectfully keep an open mind amidst venturing through new ideologies or beliefs that may be introductory to you. A little about me – I'm a 16 year old junior at CTEC High School, and I aspire to lead you toward Jesus Christ through my work in creative writing. A couple years ago, I found myself standing at the crossroads of confusion, torn between the conflicting currents of my past.Before I surrendered my life to Christ, my days were marked by the unpredictable waves of chaos. Some days, I felt ready to conquer the world; others, I was weighed down by the burdens of existence, unsure of my purpose. The dichotomy of my upbringing mirrored the turmoil within. A Christ-centered home with my mom stood in stark contrast to the absence of the Holy Spirit at my dad's house, a divide that fueled arguments and left me spiritually adrift. The early scars of my parents' divorce compounded the struggle, casting shadows over my understanding of faith. Amidst this internal conflict, I grappled with personal demons. A descent into the depths of sin, coupled with an internalized anger, threatened to drown me. Struggling with the shadows of my actions, I often lashed out, unknowingly hurting those closest to me. My journey with Christ began in the turbulence of childhood. Introduced to various perspectives on God, I decided to follow Christ at the age of 11, yet it remained a hollow commitment. Years later, amid sin and strife, I rediscovered the profound truth that God is the only source of true peace. As I matured, experiences at camp and within my church unveiled the character of the God I serve. At 14, I chose to re-dedicate my life to Christ, setting in motion a transformative process. God, in His infinite grace, revealed my fear of abandonment and the need for His love to bring mental peace. This ongoing journey has illuminated the indispensable role of God in my everyday life. Through a blossoming relationship with Christ, the importance of community, and a pivotal role in Student Leadership, I understand my purpose. God, in His boundless love, is reshaping my mentality from self-centeredness to a profound awareness of my impact on the world around me. I share this not as a singular example, but as a testament to the universal truth that God can use anyone, no matter their struggles. As you turn the pages of this book, may you discover, as I have, that in God's love, you are valued, you are cherished, and you are never alone. My name is Gibson, and I have a new life in

Christ – a life filled with purpose, love, and the unwavering presence of the Divine.

In the pages that follow, this book seeks to unfold a tapestry of crucial life lessons, each intricately woven into the fabric of my journey with God. More than a personal narrative, this is an exploration of the profound love and purpose that God has for each one of us. At the core of this journey is the revelation of God's unwavering and unconditional love. No matter the depths of our struggles or the heights of our triumphs, God's love remains a constant, a source of solace, and an anchor in the stormy seas of life. As I share the chapters of my life, forgiveness, and redemption emerge as transformative forces. God's love extends beyond our mistakes, offering the chance for redemption and the strength to forgive ourselves and others.

Life is replete with storms – trials, tribulations, and unforeseen challenges. Through my experiences, we will delve into the lessons of resilience, faith, and trust in God's guidance as we navigate the tempests that life inevitably brings. Each one of us is crafted with a purpose, intricately designed by the Creator. We will explore the importance of seeking God's plan for our lives, understanding that His purpose far surpasses our aspirations, leading us to a fulfilling and meaningful existence. A relationship with God is not a distant concept but an intimate journey. I will share insights on cultivating a deeper connection with the Divine, through prayer, meditation on His Word, and an open heart ready to receive His guidance. God designed us for fellowship and community.

Through the highs and lows of my journey, we will explore the significance of surrounding ourselves with a supportive community of believers, drawing strength and encouragement from one another. In the crucible of life's challenges, God can transform our pain into a powerful purpose. As we navigate through the struggles, we will uncover the potential for growth, healing, and the ability to be a beacon of hope for others. God's love propels us towards selfless service. We will delve into the joy that comes from aligning our lives with God's purpose and serving others with love, compassion, and humility. As you engage with these life lessons, may the wisdom gleaned from my journey serve as a guide, pointing you toward the profound truth that you are cherished and loved by a God whose purpose for your life is unique and extraordinary. May this book be a testament to the transformative power of God's love, inspiring you to embrace your journey with faith, hope, and an unwavering trust in the boundless love of our Creator.

1

Unveiling the Essence of the Gospel

In the sacred pages of the Bible, the Gospel unfolds as a profound narrative, revealing the very heart of God and His redemptive plan for humanity. Before we embark on the exploration of life lessons and issues, it is essential to delve into the core of the Gospel story — a story that shapes the very fabric of our faith. The Gospel, derived from the Old English word "godspel" or "good news," encapsulates the message of salvation and hope. At its foundational core is the story of creation, where God, in His infinite wisdom and love, crafted the world and all that is within it. Humanity, fashioned in His image, was intended for a harmonious relationship with the Creator. Yet, the human journey took a tumultuous turn. In the Garden of Eden, the first humans, Adam and Eve, succumbed to the allure of disobedience, introducing sin into the world. This disobedience ruptured the harmonious relationship between humanity and God, creating a chasm that only divine intervention could bridge. Throughout the Old Testament, God establishes covenants with His people, offering glimpses of His character and revealing His plan for redemption. From the covenant with Abraham to the giving of the Law through Moses, God's interaction with humanity laid the groundwork for the ultimate act of redemption. The pinnacle of the Gospel story is the incarnation — the divine becoming human in the person of Jesus Christ. Born of a virgin, Jesus entered the world to fulfill the long-awaited promise of a Savior. His life on Earth, marked by teachings of love, compassion, and divine authority, showcased the very nature of God. The climax of the Gospel narrative is the sacrificial death of Jesus on the cross. In an act of unparalleled love, Jesus bore the weight of humanity's sins, bridging the gap created by disobedience. The shedding of His blood became the ultimate atonement, offering reconciliation between God and humanity. The story, however, does not end at the cross. On the third day, Jesus conquered death through His resurrection. This triumphant event affirmed His divinity and signaled victory over sin and death. The resurrection became the cornerstone of the Christian faith, offering hope and eternal life to all who believe. Following His resurrection, Jesus commissioned His disciples to spread the Gospel to all nations. The Great Commission became a call to share the good news of salvation, inviting people to turn from their sins and embrace the grace offered through faith in Christ. Before ascending to heaven, Jesus promised the Holy Spirit to empower and guide believers. The birth of the early Christian Church marked the continuation of God's redemptive plan, as the Gospel message spread throughout the known world. Understanding the Gospel is foundational to navigating life's challenges and deriving meaning from its lessons. It is the story of God's relentless pursuit of a relationship with His creation, a story that culminates in the transformative power of love, redemption, and eternal hope. As we journey forward, may the profound truths of the Gospel illuminate our path, shaping our perspectives and responses to the complexities of life.

In the cosmic masterpiece painted by the Creator, the Gospel stands as a brilliant stroke of divine artistry, weaving through the vast expanse of time with hues of creation, echoes of the fall, redemptive crescendos, and the triumphant resurrection. This narrative is not a mere recounting of events; it is a symphony that resonates in the deepest chambers of the human soul, inviting us to immerse ourselves in its captivating melody. Picture, if you will, the breathtaking scene of creation — a celestial ballet where galaxies pirouette, and constellations perform a cosmic sonnet. In this grand spectacle, Earth emerges as a sacred canvas, brushed with the vibrant colors of life. Humanity, the magnum opus, stands as a testament to the Creator's boundless imagination and love, each person a living poem penned by the Divine. Yet, the serene portrait of creation finds itself disrupted in the enchanting garden of Eden. Imagine the fragility of innocence shattered as the first humans, Adam and Eve, succumb to the allure of forbidden knowledge. The once-harmonious melody now carries the dissonant notes of disobedience, and the need for redemption becomes an urgent undertone in the symphony of existence. In response to this cosmic discord, God orchestrates a series of covenants — sacred promises that echo through the corridors of time. Envision the covenant with Abraham as a celestial constellation, outlining a divine lineage through which redemption will course. The covenant with Moses unfurls like a sacred scroll, inscribing moral precepts to guide humanity back to righteousness. Each covenant, a musical motif, foreshadows the grand crescendo awaiting its moment in the Gospel symphony. Now, let the scene shift to a humble stable in Bethlehem, where the divine Composer enters the earthly stage. The incarnation, a divine melody played on the strings of humanity, resonates with the transformative teachings of Jesus Christ. His words, like a celestial sonnet, pierce through the darkness of ignorance, illuminating the path of love, compassion, and internal transformation. Fast forward to the climactic movement — the crucifixion on Calvary's hill. Visualize the cross as a bridge spanning the cosmic abyss between God and humanity. Jesus, the sinless maestro, conducts a symphony of sacrifice, offering himself as the ultimate composition of redemption. The melody of grace swells, drowning the dissonance of sin, and the cross becomes a transcendent instrument of divine reconciliation. Now, as dawn breaks over the tomb, envision the resurrection as a radiant sunrise, dispelling the shadows of death. The stone, rolled away, echoes the triumphant chords of victory over sin and the grave. Jesus, the risen Conductor, invites believers to join the harmonious dance of a resurrected life — a life immersed in hope, transformation, and eternal significance. The Great Commission reverberates like a celestial call to the farthest reaches of the universe. Imagine the Gospel as a cosmic ripple, reaching every corner of the cosmos, inviting all nations to dance to the rhythm of divine love. The Holy Spirit, like a gentle breeze, carries this transformative melody, ensuring that the symphony of redemption continues to play in the hearts of individuals and communities. As we journey through the symphony of the Gospel, it is not merely a story to be heard but a masterpiece to be experienced. The Gospel invites us to a front-row seat in the grand theater of God's love, where every note, every movement, paints a portrait of redemption. May this divine symphony resonate in the depths of our souls, transforming us into living melodies that echo the everlasting love of the Composer.

2

Redemption's Overture

In the early movements of my life's narrative, the first notes resonated with a kind of dissonance that I believe many can relate to. It's the tune of navigating adolescence, wrestling with family fractures, and trying to find my footing in matters of faith. Amid this symphony of uncertainty, there were brief moments of clarity—like rays of sunlight breaking through stormy clouds, offering a glimpse of hope. As my life's melody unfolded, darker undertones emerged. The haunting strains of my battles with personal struggles, particularly with the thorny issue of pornography, became a somber refrain. These struggles manifested externally, casting shadows over relationships, especially with my mother, where the tunes of anger and guilt played sorrowful chords. The decision to embrace Christ during my youth lacked the depth necessary for a profound journey of faith. The subsequent years unfolded as a superficial tune, more about religious rituals than cultivating a genuine relationship with the Divine. Yet, amid the wild and untamed landscape of my shortcomings, a divine light broke through. God's infinite grace led me to transformative experiences within the camp and the church community. The wilderness of confusion began to transform into sacred ground, where the seeds of redemption took root and began to grow. God's relentless pursuit unveiled the broken chords resonating with my fear of abandonment and unmet longings for love. These deep-seated issues, once shrouded in darkness, became focal points of God's transformative work. His love penetrated the recesses of my soul, healing wounds that fueled past struggles and initiating a profound transformation. In the process of rebuilding, I discovered the importance of surrender and allowing God to assume the conductor's role. The discord of sin and past mistakes were not discarded but repurposed, becoming raw materials for a melody of redemption. God's forgiveness and grace, like a masterful Composer, orchestrated a harmonious arrangement from the broken chords of my past. As I stand on the precipice of my ongoing journey, I want you, dear reader, to know that this symphony is far from complete. God's transformative work continues, and each new day presents opportunities for redemption. The mistakes of my past, now repurposed stepping stones, guide me toward a deeper understanding of God's love and purpose. So, as we journey together through these chapters, I invite you to witness the transformative power of God's redemption. Through the valleys of sin, the peaks of revelation, and the plains of rebuilding, the consistent theme persists — God turns the darkest melodies into songs of redemption. I hope that this chapter of my life resonates with yours, serving as a testament to the boundless love that transforms brokenness into a melody of grace and restoration.

In the shadowy corners of personal struggle, my life's symphony echoes with the dissonant chords of addiction. The haunting allure of pornography wasn't just a fleeting temptation but a relentless force that gripped my soul, leaving me ensnared in a web of guilt and powerlessness. It felt like an inescapable labyrinth, and perhaps you've felt the same. The constant struggle, the internal conflict, the desire for freedom – it's a symphony of battles. Here's the raw truth: addiction often thrives in isolation. It whispers lies, making you believe that you're alone in this struggle. But let me share something profound that I discovered amidst this turmoil. In the depths of my addiction, as I felt the weight of guilt and shame, there was a relentless love pursuing me. It wasn't a distant God, disapproving of my struggles; it was a God drawing near, offering a way out. So, if you find yourself entangled in the same struggle, let me speak directly to you. God's love is not a distant concept; it's a transformative force ready to meet you during your battle. It's an invitation to vulnerability, to bring your struggles into the light, to let go of the shame that keeps you in chains. Finding God's love amidst the battle isn't about perfection; it's about embracing grace. Now, let's talk about mental health battles – the silent struggles that often go unnoticed. Anxiety, depression, self-doubt – they weave a complex symphony within, and perhaps you've found yourself entangled in these intricate notes. In the throes of anxiety, God's love offers a peace that surpasses understanding. In the depths of depression, His love becomes a source of hope, a light shining in the darkness. If self-doubt is drowning out the melody of self-acceptance, God's love whispers affirmations of your worth. Broken relationships can be a source of deep wounds, and the strains of those broken chords resonate within the symphony of your life. I've been there, wrestling with anger, experiencing strained interactions, feeling the weight of fractured connections. Amidst this, God's love isn't just a theoretical concept; it's a healing balm. It's an invitation to reconciliation, a promise that broken relationships can be transformed. Self-worth struggles, the relentless pursuit of perfection, the comparisons that steal your joy – they contribute to a turbulent inner landscape. I know how it feels to drown in the dissonant whispers of inadequacy. Yet, God's love speaks directly into the depths of your identity crisis. It's a love that says you are accepted, valued, and cherished just as you are. Grief and loss – they create a symphony of sorrow that often feels unbearable. The ache of separation, the silent grieving process, the unanswered questions – they resonate deeply. In these moments, God's love isn't distant; it's a comforting melody, assuring you that even in the face of loss, His love transcends time and space. Doubt, is the subtle undercurrent that runs through the symphony, questioning faith and pondering life's mysteries. I've grappled with uncertainties and wrestled with doubts. In these moments, God's love isn't silent; it's a gentle whisper, inviting you to explore the depths of faith with authenticity. So, dear friend, wherever you find yourself in this symphony of struggles, know that God's love is not a distant concept but a present reality. It's an invitation to engage, to bring your battles into the light, and to experience a transformative love that can harmonize even the most dissonant chords of your life. Embrace grace, accept love, and journey towards the melodies of redemption that God is composing uniquely in your story.

3

Pitfalls on the Path to Redemption

In the unfolding chapters of our lives, the journey towards redemption is nuanced and intricate. As we navigate the symphony of struggles, we must recognize the pitfalls that can derail us on the path to redemption. Let's embark on this exploration together, learning from the discordant notes I've encountered and understanding the cautionary tales that can guide us away from potential pitfalls. One of the first pitfalls on the road to redemption is the illusion of self-reliance. It's tempting to believe that we can orchestrate our salvation, relying solely on our strength and willpower. Yet, I've learned that the more I tried to overcome my struggles in isolation, the further I veered from the harmonious melody of redemption. Redemption isn't a solo performance; it's a collaborative symphony with the Divine. Avoid the trap of self-reliance, and instead, embrace the transformative power of surrender. Another pitfall that I encountered was the tendency to hide behind masks of perfection. The fear of judgment and the desire to be accepted often lead us to present a curated version of ourselves, concealing the struggles beneath a façade of perfection. I've worn these masks, and they only served to deepen the dissonance within. True redemption calls for authenticity. It's about removing the masks and allowing God's love to shine on the raw, unfiltered truth of our lives. In the pursuit of redemption, it's easy to fall into the trap of chasing temporary fixes. Whether it's seeking solace in unhealthy relationships, numbing the pain with substances, or grasping for instant gratification, these shortcuts often lead to a cycle of deeper struggles. I've experienced the fleeting relief that comes from these temporary fixes, only to find myself back in the throes of discord. True redemption requires patience and a commitment to the transformative process, avoiding the allure of quick but unsustainable solutions. Isolation is a silent saboteur on the journey to redemption. I've learned that attempting to navigate the symphony of struggles alone diminishes the richness of the melody. Ignoring the power of community, whether through pride, shame, or fear of vulnerability, hinders the transformative work that God's love seeks to accomplish. Embracing a supportive community is not a sign of weakness but a testament to the strength that comes from shared journeys. On the road to redemption, self-compassion is a vital instrument that we often neglect. The relentless pursuit of perfection can lead to self-condemnation when we stumble. I've found that redemption requires a gentle and compassionate approach towards ourselves. God's love extends grace and forgiveness, and we must learn to do the same. Neglecting self-compassion hinders the harmonious interplay of redemption in our lives. Forgiveness, both seeking and extending it, is a cornerstone of redemption. I've witnessed the transformative power of forgiveness in my journey. Yet, the pitfall lies in overlooking its significance. Holding onto grudges, whether towards others or ourselves, disrupts the melody of redemption. Learning to forgive, just as we've been forgiven, is essential for the symphony to flow harmoniously. As we explore these cautionary tales, let's navigate the road to redemption with humility and openness. Each pitfall is an opportunity for growth, a chance to refine the symphony of our lives. May our journey together unveil the wisdom needed to sidestep these pitfalls and embrace the transformative love that guides us toward true redemption.

Pitfall 1: The Illusion of Self-Reliance

In the journey toward redemption, the first pitfall lies in the illusion of self-reliance. This deceptive mirage convinces individuals that they can navigate life's intricate terrain, weather its storms, and orchestrate their salvation without the need for external guidance or divine intervention. I've treaded the treacherous path of self-reliance, believing that the strength within me could withstand life's adversities. Little did I realize that this illusion was a shadowy pitfall, leading me away from the transformative melody of redemption. The allure of self-reliance often stems from societal ideals that champion independence and individual strength. It's a narrative ingrained in the cultural fabric, suggesting that vulnerability is a sign of weakness, and true strength lies in the ability to stand alone. I, too, succumbed to this illusion, attempting to traverse the complexities of life as a lone adventurer. This mirage presents itself in various forms, each luring individuals into a false sense of control. It could be the belief that one can conquer personal struggles through sheer willpower, or the notion that independence is the key to a fulfilling life. I've grappled with these illusions, thinking that my efforts alone could untangle the intricate knots of my struggles. The journey of self-reliance often starts with a desire for autonomy and control. It promises a sense of empowerment, the ability to shape one's destiny according to personal will. However, the deceptive allure of this pitfall becomes evident when faced with life's unpredictable twists and turns. It's like embarking on a solo expedition in a vast wilderness without a map, convinced that one's internal compass is enough to navigate the complexities of the terrain. I've felt the weight of this illusion during moments of personal crises. The belief that I could bear the burdens of life on my shoulders led to a sense of isolation. It's akin to standing in the center of a storm, convinced that sheer determination and resilience can withstand the raging winds. Yet, in the solitude of this storm, the dissonance became apparent – a discordant symphony drowning out the transformative melody of redemption. The pitfall of self-reliance often becomes more pronounced during times of adversity. It's in the face of challenges, be it personal struggles, relational conflicts, or existential questioning, that the mirage begins to fade. The illusion shatters, revealing the limitations of individual strength in the grand tapestry of life. One of the subtle dangers of self-reliance is the isolation it breeds. The belief that one can handle everything alone can lead to a reluctance to seek help or share vulnerabilities. I've experienced this isolation, where the fear of appearing weak or incapable prevented me from reaching out to others for support. The result was a lonely journey, far removed from the collaborative dance of redemption. Redemption, as I came to realize, is not a solo performance. It's a symphony where the individual notes of our efforts harmonize with the overarching melody of divine grace. The pitfall of self-reliance obscures this harmonious interplay, convincing individuals that they must carry the weight of their struggles alone. In the realm of faith, the illusion of self-reliance can manifest as a belief that personal righteousness or religious observance alone can secure redemption. This narrow perspective limits the transformative power of divine grace and turns the journey of faith into a checklist of individual deeds. I've grappled with this misconception, realizing that true redemption involves a surrender to the divine orchestrator rather than a reliance on personal merits. The pitfall of self-reliance also manifests in the realm of personal growth. The belief that one can navigate the journey of self-discovery and transformation without external influences or divine guidance hinders the depth of the transformative process. It's akin to trying to build a ship to sail the seas of self-discovery without acknowledging the need for the divine wind to fill its sails. In the grand tapestry of life, the illusion of self-reliance becomes a thread that, if left unexamined, weaves a discordant pattern. It's a pitfall that undermines the collaborative dance of redemption, preventing individuals from fully embracing the transformative power of divine grace. Breaking free from the illusion of self-reliance involves a fundamental shift in perspective. It requires acknowledging the limitations of individual strength and embracing the idea that true empowerment comes from a collaborative effort with the divine orchestrator. It's like realizing that the vast wilderness of life is better navigated with a guide who knows the terrain intimately. I've learned that the antidote to the pitfall of self-reliance is a humble surrender. It's recognizing that, in the grand symphony of life, our efforts are essential notes, but the transformative melody emerges when we allow the divine conductor to guide the composition. Redemption is not about standing alone in the storm but about dancing with the divine amid life's challenges. The journey towards breaking free from the pitfall of self-reliance involves a willingness to be vulnerable. It's about reaching out for support, acknowledging one's need for guidance, and embracing the interconnectedness of the human experience. It's like discovering that the collaborative dance of redemption is a communal celebration where the strength of one enhances the strength of all. As I reflect on my journey through the pitfalls of self-reliance, I recognize the moments when the illusion began to dissipate. It was in the moments of surrender, in acknowledging my need for divine guidance, that the transformative melody of redemption started to resonate more profoundly. It's a continual process of unlearning the cultural narratives of independence and embracing the truth that redemption is a collaborative dance. In the intricate dance of life, the pitfall of self-reliance is a stumbling block that, when recognized and navigated, paves the way for a more profound experience of redemption. It's a journey of letting go of the illusion that we can navigate life's challenges in isolation and opening ourselves to the transformative power of divine grace. The symphony of redemption gains richness when we relinquish the solo performance and allow the collaborative dance with the divine orchestrator to take center stage.

Thinking we can go it alone in life is like wandering a city without a map. Lost in the mess of struggles, following the misleading signs of self-reliance, I veered away from the transformative melody of redemption. Trying to cook up a perfect life with self-reliance as the main ingredient? Bitter taste. Redemption, like a flavorful dish, needs a blend of our efforts and the divine touch, creating a melody beyond our limited kitchen. Self-reliance as a stubborn solo player in a symphony? Jarring dissonance. Redemption is a collaborative effort, with each instrument—human and divine—playing a crucial role in a harmonious masterpiece. A solitary actor on a stage, claiming the spotlight? Missing the richness of sharing with the divine playwright. Redemption is a collaborative drama where the divine script enhances the narrative. The illusion of self-reliance as a stubborn weed in life's garden? Futile cultivation. The garden flourishes when divine rain showers grace our efforts, nurturing the seeds of transformation. Self-reliance is like finding your way without a compass in life's vast landscape. Wandering, redemption isn't about navigating alone but following the compass of divine guidance. Not a directionless wander, but a journey where the divine compass points the way through life's intricate landscape. Ditch the idea that we can do it all by ourselves. Redemption is a collaborative dance, a shared journey where our steps harmonize with the divine, creating a melody that resonates. It's not about perfection but connection, a shared rhythm in the messy, beautiful dance of life.

Pitfall 2: Hiding Behind the Masks of Perfection

The pursuit of perfection is a treacherous path, often laden with unrealistic expectations, hidden struggles, and the relentless pressure to present an impeccable facade to the world. It's a pitfall that many, including myself, have stumbled into, believing that projecting an image of flawlessness is the key to acceptance, worthiness, and, ultimately, redemption. The Bible offers profound insights into the illusion of perfection and the importance of authenticity. In Matthew 23:27-28, Jesus rebukes the religious leaders of his time, likening them to "whitewashed tombs" that appear beautiful on the outside but are filled with hypocrisy and wickedness within. This metaphor reveals the danger of projecting an external image of righteousness while neglecting inner transformation. In my journey, the pursuit of perfection manifested as a constant striving to meet societal standards, seeking validation through achievements, and crafting a facade that concealed internal struggles. The masks of perfection became shields, shielding vulnerabilities and imperfections from the judgment of others and, perhaps more significantly, from God. This pursuit often stems from societal pressures that equate worth with external accomplishments and flawless presentation. The cultural narrative applauds self-sufficiency, independence, and an idealized image of success. It's a narrative that I internalized, leading to a disconnection from my authentic self and an overemphasis on external validation. The illusion of perfection is like a meticulously crafted tapestry, each thread representing an aspect of the idealized self. I wove this tapestry, thread by thread, attempting to create an image that would garner approval and affirmation. However, beneath the surface, the threads were woven with the insecurities, doubts, and struggles that remained hidden from the world. The pursuit of perfection often creates a chasm between the projected self and the true self. It's like standing on a stage, performing a role meticulously scripted to meet external expectations, while the authentic self remains backstage, yearning for acknowledgment and acceptance. The dissonance between the projected image and the internal reality creates a barrier to experiencing the transformative power of redemption. The Bible challenges this illusion by emphasizing the value of authenticity and vulnerability. Proverbs 28:13 declares, "Whoever conceals their sins does not prosper, but the one who confesses and renounces them finds mercy." This verse underscores the importance of acknowledging and confessing imperfections rather than concealing them behind a facade of perfection. In my journey, the breakthrough came when I began to unravel the tapestry of perfection and embrace vulnerability. It involved a courageous admission of struggles, a willingness to be seen authentically, and a recognition that redemption is not found in flawless presentation but in the transformative work of divine grace. The pursuit of perfection often stems from a deep-seated fear of judgment and rejection. It's like constructing a fortress around the vulnerable self, fortifying it against the perceived threats of criticism and disapproval. However, this fortress becomes a self-imposed prison, hindering the free flow of divine grace and the transformative power of redemption. The Bible encourages believers to approach God with authenticity and humility. Psalm 51:17 expresses, "The sacrifices of God are a broken spirit; a broken and contrite heart, O God, you will not despise." This verse highlights the divine receptivity to the authentic, broken self—the self that acknowledges imperfections and seeks the transformative touch of divine mercy. Breaking free from the pitfall of perfection involves dismantling the masks, tearing down the fortress, and allowing the authentic self to step into the light. It's a journey of self-discovery that acknowledges the beauty in imperfection, the value in vulnerability, and the transformative potential in the divine encounter. The pursuit of perfection often leads to a relentless cycle of achievement, where each success becomes a fleeting moment of validation, quickly overshadowed by the pressure to maintain a flawless image. It's like chasing an elusive mirage, always one step away from satisfaction, and never fully experiencing the transformative embrace of divine acceptance. The Bible offers a counter-narrative, inviting individuals to rest in the assurance of God's unconditional love. In Matthew 11:28-30, Jesus extends an invitation, saying, "Come to me, all you who are weary and burdened, and I will give you rest. Take my yoke upon you and learn from me, for I am gentle and humble in heart, and you will find rest for your souls." This invitation is a call to release the burdens of perfection and find solace in the transformative rest offered by God's grace. In my journey, the realization that perfection is an unattainable mirage brought a sense of liberation. It involved a shift from the relentless pursuit of external validation to a journey of self-acceptance rooted in divine love. The transformative power of redemption became evident as I embraced the imperfect self and allowed God's grace to work in the brokenness. Breaking free from the illusion of perfection requires a shift in perspective—an acknowledgment that redemption is not found in flawless presentation but in an honest, authentic encounter with God. It's a journey of letting go of the masks, dismantling the fortress and allowing the transformative touch of divine grace to weave a new tapestry—one that celebrates the beauty in imperfection and reflects the authentic self embraced by God's unconditional love.

Pitfall 3: Chasing Temporary Fixes

The third pitfall on the journey toward redemption involves the perilous pursuit of temporary fixes. In our quest for relief from pain, satisfaction at the moment, or an escape from internal struggles, we often turn to quick, ephemeral solutions that offer temporary gratification but fail to address the root causes of our challenges. This pitfall, which I've personally encountered, leads individuals down a maze of instant gratification, diverting them from the transformative healing that true redemption provides. The Bible provides valuable insights into the dangers of seeking transient pleasures without considering their long-term consequences. Proverbs 14:12 warns, "There is a way that appears to be right, but in the end, it leads to death." This proverb serves as a cautionary tale, emphasizing the importance of discernment in choosing paths that lead to lasting fulfillment rather than momentary satisfaction. The pursuit of temporary fixes is akin to attempting to quench an insatiable thirst with drops of water, each sip offering a fleeting sense of relief but ultimately leaving the deeper longing unfulfilled. It's a journey that often involves chasing after mirages—illusions of contentment that vanish upon closer inspection, revealing the barrenness of the terrain. One common avenue for chasing temporary fixes is through the allure of hedonistic pleasures, where individuals seek immediate gratification in the form of sensual or material indulgence. This pursuit may involve the consumption of substances, engaging in impulsive behaviors, or seeking pleasure in relationships without considering the consequences. The Bible addresses the dangers of succumbing to hedonistic pursuits without discernment. In Ecclesiastes, the author reflects on the fleeting nature of worldly pleasures, proclaiming, "I said to myself, 'Come now, I will test you with pleasure to find out what is good.' But that also proved to be meaningless" (Ecclesiastes 2:1). This reflection underscores the transient nature of hedonistic pursuits and the emptiness that ensues when they become the focal point of one's existence. In my journey, I grappled with the allure of temporary fixes, seeking solace in momentary pleasures to numb the pain or distract from internal struggles. The pursuit of instant gratification offered brief respites from the challenges I faced, but it was akin to placing bandages on wounds that required deeper healing. The quest for temporary fixes is also evident in the prevalence of instant gratification culture, where technological advancements offer immediate access to information, entertainment, and communication. While these conveniences enhance efficiency, they also contribute to a mindset that craves quick solutions and instant pleasure. The Bible challenges the notion of prioritizing immediate gratification over enduring transformation. Romans 12:2 exhorts believers to "not conform to the pattern of this world, but be transformed by the renewing of your mind." This verse encourages a shift in mindset—a departure from the quick-fix culture—and an embrace of the transformative process that redemption unfolds. Breaking free from the pitfall of chasing temporary fixes involves a shift in perspective—a recognition that lasting fulfillment is found in the transformative journey of redemption rather than in momentary pleasures. It requires discernment to distinguish between the allure of instant gratification and the deeper, more meaningful path of enduring healing. The pursuit of temporary fixes often involves an avoidance of confronting the deeper issues at hand. It's like applying a fresh coat of paint to a deteriorating structure, masking the underlying problems without addressing their root causes. This avoidance perpetuates a cycle of seeking fleeting relief without experiencing the profound changes that redemption offers. In my journey toward freedom from this pitfall, I found solace in the wisdom of Psalm 34:8, which invites individuals to "taste and see that the Lord is good; blessed is the one who takes refuge in him." This verse underscores the invitation to find true satisfaction and refuge in God, moving beyond the transient allure of temporary fixes. The pursuit of instant gratification often involves a disconnection from the present moment—a constant seeking of the next pleasure, the next distraction, or the next escape. This perpetual restlessness prevents individuals from fully engaging with the transformative opportunities presented in the present, hindering their progress toward redemption. The Bible encourages believers to embrace the concept of mindfulness and presence. Psalm 46:10 advises, "Be still, and know that I am God." This verse invites individuals to cultivate a sense of stillness, allowing them to be fully present and receptive to the transformative presence of God. Breaking free from the pitfall of chasing temporary fixes involves a conscious effort to be present, to engage with the deeper realities of one's journey, and to seek enduring solutions rather than quick escapes. In my personal experience, navigating the maze of instant gratification required a reevaluation of my priorities and a recognition that the pursuit of lasting fulfillment demanded patience and a willingness to confront the underlying issues. The temporary fixes that once seemed appealing lost their luster as I embraced the transformative journey of redemption, recognizing that true satisfaction is found in the enduring embrace of divine grace. Breaking free from the pitfall of chasing temporary fixes involves a shift in mindset—a departure from the instant gratification culture and a commitment to the transformative process of redemption. It requires discernment, mindfulness, and a willingness to confront the deeper issues at the heart of one's struggles. The journey toward lasting fulfillment is not found in the pursuit of momentary pleasures but in the transformative embrace of God's enduring love.

Pitfall 4: Neglecting the Power of Community

The fourth pitfall on the journey toward redemption involves neglecting the power of community—a tendency to isolate oneself, believing in the illusion of self-sufficiency, and underestimating the transformative impact of shared experiences within a supportive network of believers. This pitfall, which I've personally grappled with, hinders individuals from fully embracing the collective strength, encouragement, and accountability that arise from walking the journey together. The Bible places significant emphasis on the importance of community and shared experiences. Hebrews 10:24-25 encourages believers to "consider how we may spur one another on toward love and good deeds, not giving up meeting together, as some are in the habit of doing, but encouraging one another." This verse underscores the power of community in fostering spiritual growth and mutual support.

Neglecting the power of community often stems from a misconception of self-sufficiency—an illusion that one can navigate life's challenges in isolation. This mindset can lead individuals to believe they don't need the support of others, either due to a fear of vulnerability or a misguided sense of independence. However, the transformative journey toward redemption is inherently communal, requiring a network of believers who can offer encouragement, share wisdom, and provide accountability. In my journey, there were times when I resisted opening up to others about my struggles, believing that vulnerability was a sign of weakness. I convinced myself that I could overcome challenges on my own, neglecting the power of community. This mindset led to a sense of isolation, hindering the transformative impact that shared experiences within a supportive community can provide. The illusion of self-sufficiency is like attempting to navigate a dense forest without a guide. It may seem possible to forge ahead on one's own, but the journey becomes more challenging, and the likelihood of losing one's way increases. Similarly, neglecting the power of community isolates individuals on their redemptive journey, preventing them from benefiting from the collective wisdom, strength, and encouragement found in the shared experiences of fellow believers. The Bible presents the concept of the body of Christ, emphasizing the interconnectedness of believers and the importance of each member playing a unique role. In 1 Corinthians 12:12-27, the apostle Paul uses the metaphor of the body to illustrate the unity and diversity within the community of believers. This metaphor highlights the idea that every member, with their unique gifts and experiences, contributes to the overall health and vitality of the body. Neglecting the power of the community is like attempting to sever a limb from the body—a disconnection that hinders the individual and weakens the collective strength of the community. In my journey, recognizing the importance of community involved understanding that my struggles, victories, and experiences were interwoven with those of my fellow believers. It required embracing the truth that my journey toward redemption was not meant to be a solitary endeavor but a communal expression of shared faith. The transformative impact of community is evident in the power of shared testimonies. Revelation 12:11 declares, "They triumphed over him [the accuser] by the blood of the Lamb and by the word of their testimony." This verse underscores the strength found in sharing one's story within the context of a supportive community. Testimonies become a source of encouragement, inspiration, and hope, serving as a reminder that redemption is not only a personal experience but a collective journey. In my own experience, sharing my testimony within a community of believers became a pivotal moment in my redemptive journey. It was a vulnerability that led to a cascade of support, encouragement, and shared experiences from others who had walked similar paths. The power of community became a transformative force, revealing the strength that arises when believers join together in their pursuit of redemption. Neglecting the power of the community can also manifest as a fear of judgment or rejection. The vulnerability required to open up about struggles may be hindered by the apprehension that others will perceive weakness or failure. This fear often stems from societal stigmas or misconceptions about the nature of the redemptive journey. However, the Bible encourages believers to bear one another's burdens and to extend grace and support in times of need. Galatians 6:2 urges believers to "carry each other's burdens, and in this way, you will fulfill the law of Christ."

This verse emphasizes the communal responsibility to support one another through the challenges of life. Neglecting the power of community prevents individuals from experiencing the transformative exchange of burdens within a supportive network of believers. In my journey, overcoming the fear of judgment involved recognizing that true community is built on the foundation of grace and acceptance. It required understanding that vulnerability is not a sign of weakness but a courageous acknowledgment of one's humanity. The transformative impact of the community lies in the shared acceptance of imperfections and the mutual commitment to walk the redemptive journey together. Breaking free from the pitfall of neglecting the power of community involves a conscious decision to open up, connect with fellow believers, and recognize the strength found in shared experiences. It requires vulnerability, humility, and a willingness to extend and receive support within the context of a supportive community. The transformative journey toward redemption is enriched and fortified when individuals recognize the inherent strength and encouragement that arise when they walk together in a community.

Pitfall 5: Neglecting Self-Compassion

The fifth pitfall on the journey toward redemption involves neglecting self-compassion—an inclination to be overly critical of oneself, holding unrealistic expectations, and failing to extend the same grace and forgiveness to oneself that God freely offers. This pitfall creates a cycle of self-condemnation, inhibiting the transformative process of redemption. The Bible emphasizes the importance of self-compassion and grace. Romans 8:1 declares, "Therefore, there is now no condemnation for those who are in Christ Jesus." This verse underscores the freedom from self-condemnation that comes through faith in Christ. Neglecting self-compassion often stems from a distorted view of redemption, where individuals believe they must earn their way back into God's favor through perfection. This mindset perpetuates a cycle of guilt, shame, and inadequacy, hindering the transformative embrace of God's grace. The illusion that redemption requires flawless self-performance is akin to attempting to climb an infinite staircase, each step representing a perceived expectation. In my own journey, neglecting self-compassion manifested as an internal dialogue of relentless self-criticism, a constant striving for an unattainable standard. It created a barrier to fully experiencing the transformative love and acceptance that God freely offers. Breaking free from this pitfall involves recognizing that redemption is not earned through perfection but received through grace. Self-compassion requires acknowledging one's humanity, embracing imperfections, and allowing God's transformative grace to work in the midst of struggles. The transformative journey toward redemption is hindered when individuals remain ensnared in the cycle of self-condemnation, failing to extend to themselves the same forgiveness, love, and acceptance that God abundantly provides. Embracing self-compassion is a foundational step toward unlocking the fullness of redemption's transformative power, allowing individuals to experience the freedom and renewal that come through God's boundless grace.

Neglecting self-compassion is a subtle yet powerful pitfall that can entwine individuals in a web of self-criticism, guilt, and an unrelenting pursuit of an unattainable standard. This intricate pattern of neglecting oneself becomes a hindrance on the transformative journey toward redemption, preventing individuals from fully experiencing the depth of God's love, forgiveness, and transformative grace. The intricacies of this pitfall often lie in distorted perceptions of redemption, where the notion of earning God's favor through perfection takes root, perpetuating a harmful cycle of self-condemnation. Romans 8:1 stands as a beacon of truth in the midst of this pitfall, declaring, "Therefore, there is now no condemnation for those who are in Christ Jesus." Yet, the human tendency to self-condemn persists, creating a dissonance between the liberating promise of God's grace and the self-imposed burden of perfection. In my personal journey, this dissonance manifested as an internal dialogue filled with harsh self-criticism—a relentless striving to meet an elusive standard that seemed to move further away with every step. The illusion that redemption necessitates flawless self-performance is akin to attempting to climb an infinite staircase, each step representing a perceived expectation or requirement. The expectations, whether rooted in societal pressures, past mistakes, or distorted views of spirituality, become an insurmountable obstacle when they overshadow the fundamental truth that redemption is a gift freely given, not a reward earned through faultless living. Breaking free from this pitfall involves a profound shift in perspective—a recognition that redemption is not a transaction but a re-lational journey with a God who extends boundless love and forgiveness. Self-compassion, an integral aspect of this transformative process, requires acknowledging one's inher-ent humanity, embracing imperfections, and allowing God's transformative grace to work in the midst of struggles. The internal struggle against self-condemnation often begins with distorted views of God's character. The belief that God's love is contingent upon flawless performance distorts the essence of redemption, turning it into a precarious balancing act where one's worthiness is perpetually on trial. This dis-torted view of God can be traced back to various influences, including rigid religious doctrines, cultural expectations, and personal experiences that shape perceptions of divine love. In my own journey, the struggle against self-condemnation was intertwined with a deep-seated belief that God's love had to be earned through perfection. This belief led to a constant fear of falling short, of never measuring up to an arbitrary standard that overshadowed the reality of God's unconditional love. It was as if the tapestry of redemption, woven with threads of grace and forgiveness, became obscured by the shadows of unrealistic expectations. The transformative journey toward redemption necessitates a reevaluation of these distorted beliefs about God's character. It involves unraveling the threads of misconception, uncovering the true nature of divine love, and recognizing that redemption is an invitation to intimacy with a God who embraces humanity with all its flaws. Ephesians 1:7 reminds believers of the richness of God's grace, stating, "In him, we have redemption through his blood, the forgiveness of sins, in accordance with the riches of God's grace." Embracing self-compassion also involves acknowledging the impact of past mistakes without allowing them to define one's identity. The tendency to internalize past errors and wear them as a badge of shame becomes a significant barrier on the journey toward redemption. Instead of seeing mistakes as opportunities for growth and transformation, individuals ensnared in this pitfall carry the weight of self-condemnation, preventing the full realization of God's forgiveness and renewal. The transformative power of redemption is encapsulated in the idea that God's grace transcends the limitations of human shortcomings. Psalm 103:12 beautifully expresses this truth, declaring, "As far as the east is from the west, so far has he removed our transgressions from us." The imagery in this verse underscores the boundless nature of God's forgiveness, portraying a distance that cannot be measured or comprehended. In my own journey, the release from self-condemnation came through a deep understanding of the magnitude of God's forgiveness. It involved recognizing that mistakes, though significant, were not insurmountable barriers to God's love. The transformative journey required letting go of the weight of past errors and embracing the truth that redemption is not contingent upon flawless performance but on the boundless grace of a God who removes transgressions as far as the east is from the west. Self-compassion further entails allowing God's transformative grace to work within the struggles of everyday life. It is an acknowledgment that the journey toward redemption is not a linear path of perfection but a process of growth and refinement. The pitfall of neglecting self-compassion often leads individuals to resist vulnerability, fearing that revealing struggles will diminish their worthiness. However, vulnerability is the bridge that connects the human experience with the transformative power of God's love. The Bible affirms the strength found in vulnerability, with 2 Corinthians 12:9 declaring, "But he said to me, 'My grace is sufficient for you, for my power is made perfect in weakness.'" This verse encapsulates the paradox that divine strength is revealed in moments of human weakness. In my own journey, embracing vulnerability became a catalyst for the transformative work of redemption. It involved sharing struggles, acknowledging weaknesses, and recognizing that God's grace is not contingent upon having it all together. The transformative journey toward redemption is not about presenting a facade of perfection but about allowing God's power to manifest in the midst of human frailty. Breaking free from the pitfall of neglecting self-compassion is a continual process that requires a deliberate shift in mindset. It involves dismantling the internal dialogue of self-condemnation, challenging distorted views of God's character, and embracing vulnerability as a gateway to divine strength. The transformative journey toward redemption becomes a profound exploration of God's boundless love and the recognition that self-compassion is not only an essential aspect of personal healing but a testament to the richness of God's grace.

Pitfall 6: Overlooking the Transformative Power of Forgiveness

The next pitfall on the journey toward redemption involves overlooking the transformative power of forgiveness. It is a perilous oversight that can impede the healing process, perpetuating cycles of resentment, guilt, and relational brokenness. The Bible places a profound emphasis on the importance of forgiveness, with Ephesians 4:32 urging believers to "be kind and compassionate to one another, forgiving each other, just as in Christ God forgave you." This verse underscores the reciprocity of forgiveness—receiving divine forgiveness and extending it to others. Overlooking the transformative power of forgiveness often stems from a misunderstanding of its nature. It is not merely an act of pardoning wrongdoing but a dynamic process that involves releasing the burdens of resentment, embracing empathy, and fostering reconciliation. In my own journey, the failure to recognize the transformative potential of forgiveness led to harboring grudges, clinging to past hurts, and perpetuating a cycle of relational strife. The illusion that withholding forgiveness provides a sense of control is akin to holding onto a heavy burden, falsely believing that it shields from vulnerability. The transformative journey toward redemption requires a willingness to unpack the layers of unforgiveness, acknowledging the weight they impose and recognizing the freedom found in releasing them. Forgiveness is an intricate tapestry that interweaves threads of empathy, understanding, and grace. It involves acknowledging the pain caused, understanding the humanity of the offender, and choosing to release the grip of bitterness. The Bible illustrates this transformative process in the parable of the unforgiving servant (Matthew 18:21-35), where a servant, forgiven of a significant debt, fails to extend the same mercy to a fellow servant. The parable underscores the transformative power of forgiveness and the consequences of neglecting to extend it to others. In my journey of grappling with this pitfall, the turning point came when I recognized that forgiveness is not a condoning of the wrong but a release of the hold it has on one's heart. It involved understanding that extending forgiveness is a gift to oneself—a step toward personal healing and liberation from the chains of resentment. The transformative journey toward redemption necessitates a shift from viewing forgiveness as a transactional act to perceiving it as a relational and internal transformation. It requires acknowledging the complexity of human relationships, understanding the impact of wounds inflicted, and choosing a path of healing and restoration. The transformative power of forgiveness becomes evident in the restoration of fractured relationships and the liberation from the emotional shackles of unforgiveness. Overlooking this transformative aspect of forgiveness perpetuates a cycle of relational brokenness, hindering the full experience of redemption in both personal and communal contexts. The Bible underscores the communal dimension of forgiveness, with Colossians 3:13 urging believers to "bear with each other and forgive one another if any of you has a grievance against someone. Forgive as the Lord forgave you." This verse emphasizes the interconnectedness of forgiveness within the community of believers and the reciprocal nature of extending the grace of forgiveness received from God. In my own journey, the recognition of forgiveness as a communal and reciprocal practice led to a deepened understanding of its transformative power. It involved not only seeking forgiveness from others but also extending forgiveness, recognizing that the journey toward redemption is enriched when forgiveness becomes a shared experience within the community. Breaking free from the pitfall of overlooking the transformative power of forgiveness requires a deliberate commitment to cultivating a forgiving heart. It involves acknowledging the wounds, extending empathy to those who have caused harm, and choosing the path of reconciliation. The transformative journey toward redemption becomes a testament to the richness of God's forgiveness, an embodiment of divine grace within human relationships. It is a continual process of releasing the burdens of unforgiveness, embracing the transformative power of forgiveness, and allowing the redemptive grace of God to weave a new tapestry of healed and reconciled relationships.

4

═══

Threading the Needle

In the culmination of this transformative journey toward redemption, it is essential to weave together the threads of understanding, growth, and faith that have been explored throughout this book. The transformative power of redemption, intricately portrayed in the stories of individuals grappling with various pitfalls, finds its roots in the timeless wisdom of the Bible. As we stand at the precipice of concluding this journey, let us embark on a comprehensive exploration of the lessons learned and the profound implications for your next steps as a believer. The journey toward redemption has unfolded as a tapestry, intricately woven with threads of grace, forgiveness, community, and self-compassion. Each pitfall explored has revealed both the common struggles faced by believers and the transformative power inherent in overcoming these challenges. The narrative arcs of personal stories, anchored in biblical principles, provide a profound illustration of the redemptive journey that transcends individual experiences. The Bible, as the foundational guide, has consistently illuminated the path toward redemption. Ephesians 1:7 beautifully captures the essence of this journey, declaring, "In him, we have redemption through his blood, the forgiveness of sins, in accordance with the riches of God's grace." This verse encapsulates the core tenets of redemption – forgiveness, grace, and the transformative power of Christ's sacrifice. A pivotal theme that emerged is the transformative power of forgiveness. Ephesians 4:32 guided our exploration, urging believers to "be kind and compassionate to one another, forgiving each other, just as in Christ God forgave you." The parable of the unforgiving servant (Matthew 18:21-35) underscored the reciprocal nature of forgiveness—a theme interwoven into the fabric of redemption. Understanding forgiveness as a dynamic, transformative process is key. It is not a mere transaction but a continual journey of releasing the burdens of resentment and embracing empathy. The communal dimension of forgiveness, highlighted in Colossians 3:13, emphasizes the interconnectedness of forgiveness within the community of believers. As you reflect on your journey, consider the richness of forgiveness not only as an individual practice but as a communal experience that fosters unity and reconciliation. Each pitfall explored—the illusion of self-sufficiency, the pursuit of temporary fixes, neglecting the power of community, overlooking self-compassion, and underestimating the transformative power of forgiveness— reveals the common challenges faced by believers. Romans 8:1 echoed throughout, reminding us that "there is now no condemnation for those who are in Christ Jesus." The journey toward redemption is a transformative process that unfolds within the embrace of divine grace, liberating believers from the shackles of self-condemnation. The pitfall of neglecting self-compassion, a subtle yet powerful challenge, was addressed with a profound shift in perspective. Recognizing that redemption is not earned through perfection but received through grace is essential. Ephesians 2:8-9 reinforces this truth, declaring, "For it is by grace you have been saved, through faith—and this is not from yourselves, it is the gift of God—not by works so that no one can boast." The importance of community was a recurring theme, aligning with Hebrews 10:24-25, which urges believers to "consider how we may spur one another on toward love and good deeds, not giving up meeting together, as some are in the habit of doing, but encouraging one another." Neglecting the power of community isolates individuals on their redemptive journey, hindering the transformative impact of shared experiences, mutual support, and collective growth. Recognizing the interconnectedness of believers, as illustrated in 1 Corinthians 12:12-27, brings depth to the transformative journey. Embrace the diversity of gifts and experiences within the community, understanding that each member plays a unique role in contributing to the overall health and vitality of the body of Christ. Your next steps as a believer involve active participation in and contribution to the transformative power of community, fostering an environment where each member is supported and encouraged on their redemptive journey. As you stand at this juncture, the transformative power of redemption invites you to contemplate your next steps as a believer. Here is a comprehensive roadmap, deeply rooted in biblical principles, to guide you on your continued journey. Ground yourself in the transformative power of God's Word. Psalm 119:105 declares, "Your word is a lamp for my feet, a light on my path." Engage in daily reflection, prayer, and meditation on Scripture to navigate the intricacies of your redemptive journey. Actively practice forgiveness in your daily interactions. Matthew 6:14-15 emphasizes the reciprocal nature of forgiveness, stating, "For if you forgive other people when they sin against you, your heavenly Father will also forgive you. But if you do not forgive others their sins, your Father will not forgive your sins." Cultivating a forgiving heart aligns your journey with the transformative power of God's forgiveness. Recognize the strength found in vulnerability, both within your relationship with God and within the community of believers. 2 Corinthians 12:9 encourages believers, stating, "My grace is sufficient for you, for my power is made perfect in weakness." Embrace vulnerability as a gateway to divine strength and communal support.

Actively engage in your community of believers. Hebrews 10:24-25 underscores the importance of communal support, urging believers to "spur one another on toward love and good deeds." Your active participation contributes to the transformative power of community, fostering an environment where mutual encouragement and shared growth thrive. As you navigate the intricate weave of your redemptive journey, consider Ephesians 4:16, emphasizing that "from him the whole body, joined and held together by every supporting ligament, grows and builds itself up in love, as each part does its work." Your role within the community is integral to the collective growth and strengthening of the body of Christ. Furthermore, embrace the transformative potential of forgiveness both as an individual practice and a communal experience. Matthew 18:20 reminds believers that "where two or three gather in my name, there am I with them." As forgiveness flows within the community, the presence of God is palpable, fostering an atmosphere of unity, love, and reconciliation. Extend compassion not only to others but also to yourself, recognizing the transformative power of self-compassion. Galatians 6:2 encourages believers to "carry each other's burdens, and in this way, you will fulfill the law of Christ." Acknowledging your own vulnerabilities and extending grace to yourself aligns with the communal ethos of shared burdens and mutual support. Your next steps as a believer involve an ongoing commitment to personal growth, both spiritually and within the community. The transformative journey toward redemption is not a solitary endeavor but a collective pilgrimage, strengthened by the bonds of shared faith and mutual encouragement. In the tapestry of your redemptive journey, each thread of understanding, forgiveness, community, and self-compassion weaves together to create a vibrant, transformative narrative. May your continued steps be guided by the timeless truths of the Bible, and may you find fulfillment in contributing to the collective story of redemption within the community of believers.

Conclusion

In the culmination of this exploration into the transformative power of God's love, our collective journey unfolds as a narrative of redemption—a dynamic process woven with threads of grace, forgiveness, community, and self-compassion. Gibson Groft's personal testimony marked the starting point, reflecting the complexities of faith amidst life's challenges. From familial discord to internal struggles, his story resonates with the human experience—a journey marked by highs and lows, victories and defeats. Yet, within this narrative, a recurring theme emerges—the transformative power of God's love and the redemptive grace found in a relationship with Christ. Navigating the terrain of common challenges faced by believers, we encountered pitfalls that served as signposts guiding us toward redemption. The illusion of self-sufficiency crumbled before the truth of Ephesians 2:8-9, emphasizing our need for God's grace. The pursuit of temporary fixes yielded to the enduring truth of Romans 8:1, offering freedom from condemnation through Christ. Neglecting the power of community found resolution in the communal ethos of Hebrews 10:24-25, recognizing the transformative impact of shared experiences. Overlooking self-compassion gave way to the acknowledgment of grace within Ephesians 2:8-9, where redemption is not earned but received as a gift. The transformative power of forgiveness emerged as a central theme, echoing the biblical call to forgive as we have been forgiven (Ephesians 4:32). Within our communal journey, the interconnectedness of believers became evident. Illustrated in 1 Corinthians 12:12-27, each member contributes to the overall health and vitality of the body of Christ. The transformative power of community is not passive but active, requiring believers to engage, contribute, and encourage one another. Vulnerability, perceived as weakness, became a source of divine strength within the narrative of redemption. 2 Corinthians 12:9 invited believers to embrace vulnerability, recognizing God's power in weakness. The foundational role of God's Word emerged throughout this journey. Psalm 119:105 captured the essence of Scripture as a guiding force in navigating the redemptive journey. Engaging with God's Word became a source of wisdom, comfort, and guidance, shaping thoughts, attitudes, and actions. As believers stand at the crossroads, a roadmap for continued growth emerges—a roadmap rooted in biblical principles. Daily renewal through God's Word, cultivating a forgiving heart, embracing vulnerability within the community, and active participation in the communal journey of redemption constitute essential waypoints on this roadmap. The transformative power of these practices extends beyond individual growth to the flourishing of the entire body of Christ. In the chapters ahead, may the lessons learned and the biblical truths embraced guide believers' steps. Ephesians 4:16 reminds us that the whole body grows and builds itself up in love, as each part actively engages in the collective narrative of redemption. The journey ahead beckons with richness and depth, inviting believers to contribute their unique threads to the ongoing narrative of God's redemptive work.